al Library

Tree Frogs

by Mari Schuh

Bullfrog
Books

Ideas for Parents and Teachers

Bullfrog Books let children practice reading informational text at the earliest reading levels. Repetition, familiar words, and photo labels support early readers.

Before Reading

- Discuss the cover photo. What does it tell them?

- Look at the picture glossary together. Read and discuss the words.

Read the Book

- "Walk" through the book and look at the photos. Let the child ask questions. Point out the photo labels.

- Read the book to the child, or have him or her read independently.

After Reading

- Prompt the child to think more. Ask: Have you ever seen a frog? What color was it? Have you ever seen such a brightly colored frog?

Dedicated to David and Alex Schuh —MS

Bullfrog Books are published by Jump!
5357 Penn Avenue South
Minneapolis, MN 55419
www.jumplibrary.com

Library of Congress Cataloging-in-Publication Data
Schuh, Mari C., 1975- author.
 Tree frogs / by Mari Schuh.
     pages cm.—(My first animal library)
 Summary: "This photo-illustrated book for early readers tells the story of a tree frog's life in the rain forest"—Provided by publisher.
 Audience: Ages 5-8.
 Audience: K to grade 3.
 Includes bibliographical references and index.
 ISBN 978-1-62031-114-1 (hardcover)
 ISBN 978-1-62496-181-6 (ebook)
 1. Hylidae—Juvenile literature.
 2. Frogs--Juvenile literature. I. Title.
 QL668.E24S38 2015
 639.3'7878—dc23

                                    2013045665

Editor: Wendy Dieker
Series Designer: Ellen Huber
Book Designer: Lindaanne Donohoe
Photo Researcher: Kurtis Kinneman

Photo Credits: Biosphoto, 16–17; Dreamstime, 4; Getty Images, 20–21; iStock, 6–7, 13; Nature Picture Library, 5, 14–15; Shutterstock, cover, 1, 3 (both), 8, 9, 10–11, 12, 19, 22, 23bl, 24; SuperStock, 18–19, 20, 23tl, 23tr, 23br

Printed in the United States of America at Corporate Graphics, North Mankato, Minnesota.
6-2014
10 9 8 7 6 5 4 3 2 1

Table of Contents

Life in the Trees

The sun shines.
A tree frog sleeps.

A frog hides
on a leaf.

Can you see him?

7

Oh no! A hungry snake!

The tree frog opens his big eyes.
They are bright!

The tree frog
stretches.

He shows his
bright colors.

Surprise!

The snake goes
away.

The tree frog climbs away.
He uses sticky pads on his feet.

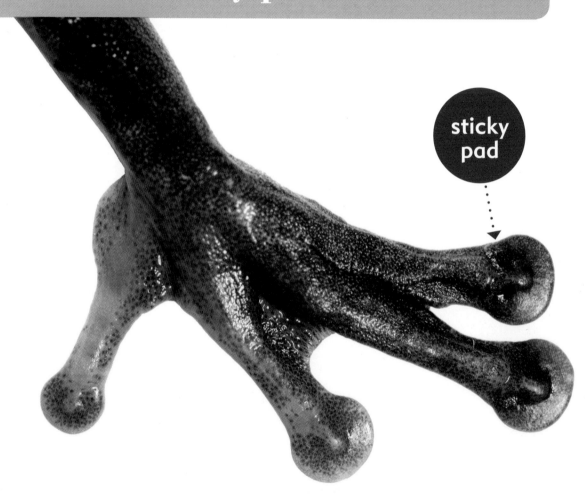

sticky pad

He sleeps again.

Night is here.

A tree frog
wakes up.

He eats an insect.

Gulp!

He wants to mate.

His throat gets
big like a bubble.

Ribbit. Ribbit.

A female hears him.

They mate.

She lays eggs in the water.

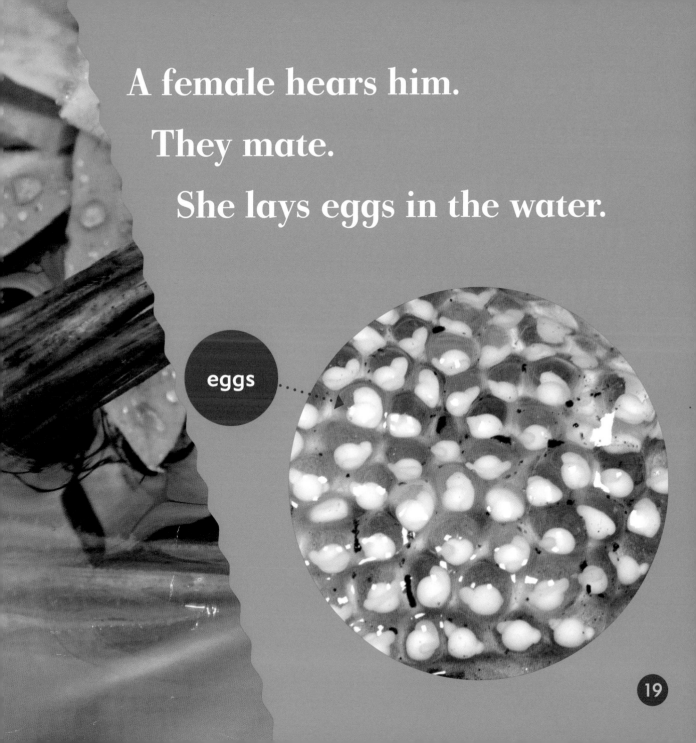

eggs

After a few days,
tadpoles hatch.

They will grow into
tree frogs.

Ribbit! Ribbit!

tadpole

Parts of a Tree Frog

eye
Big eyes help tree frogs see in the dark.

leg
Long, thin legs are better for climbing than jumping.

pad
Sticky pads on their toes help tree frogs climb.

Picture Glossary

hatch
To break out of an egg.

mate
To join together to make young.

insect
A small animal with six legs and three main body parts.

tadpole
A stage of a tree frog's life; tadpoles grow into tree frogs.

Index

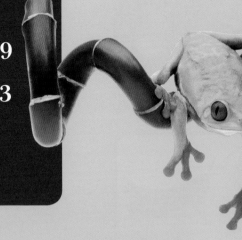

To Learn More

Learning more is as easy as 1, 2, 3.

1) Go to www.factsurfer.com

2) Enter "tree frogs" into the search box.

3) Click the "Surf" button to see a list of websites.

With factsurfer.com, finding more information is just a click away.